WELCOME TO ALL THE PLEASURES

(Ode for St Cecili

Edited by
BRUCE WOOD

PURCELL

PIANO
(Reduction and
Continuo)
for rehearsal only

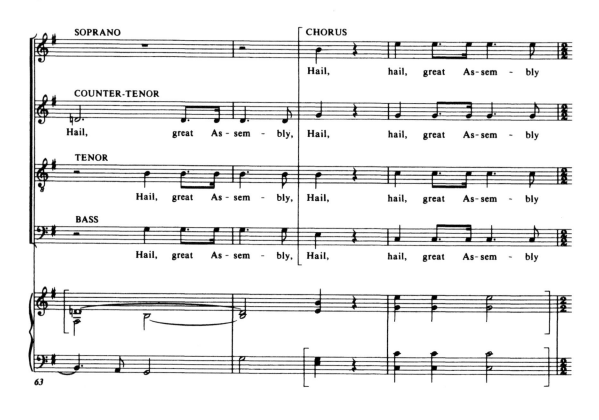

COUNTER-TENOR SOLO

Here the

12

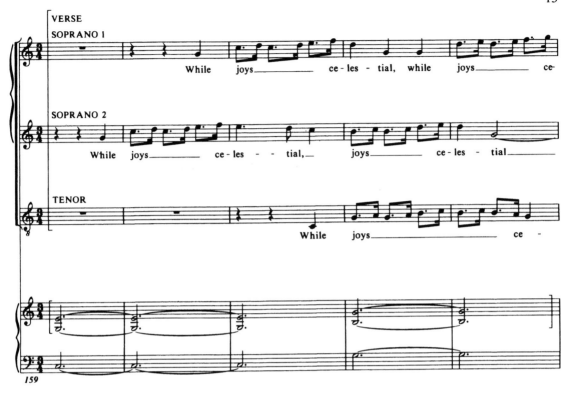

-ment you have made, While joys_____ ce - les - tial, while joys_____ ce -

-ment you have made, While joys_____ ce - les - tial, while joys_____ ce -

- ment you have made, While joys_____ ce -

169

- les - tial their_ bright souls in - vade To find___ what_ great___ im - prove-

- les - tial their bright_ souls in - vade To find what great___ im - prove-

- les - tial their bright souls in - vade To___ find what great im - prove-

174

194

199

204

BASS SOLO

Then lift up your voi - ces, those_ or - gans_ of__ Na - ture, Those charms to the

210

trou - bled and am - - - o - rous crea - ture; Then lift up your voi - ces, those

215

or - gans_ of__ Na - ture, Those charms to the trou - bled and__ am - - o - rous_

220

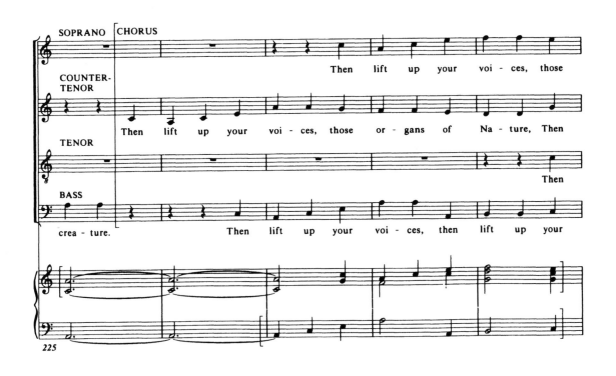

SOPRANO CHORUS

Then lift up your voi - ces, those

COUNTER-TENOR

Then lift up your voi - ces, those or - gans of Na - ture, Then

TENOR

Then

BASS

crea - ture. Then lift up your voi - ces, then lift up your

225

230

235

- bey, And love its soft_ charms, and love its soft_ charms must o - bey.

- bey, And love its soft_ charms, its soft_ charms_ must_ o - bey.

- bey, And love its soft_ charms, and love its soft_ charms must o - bey.

252

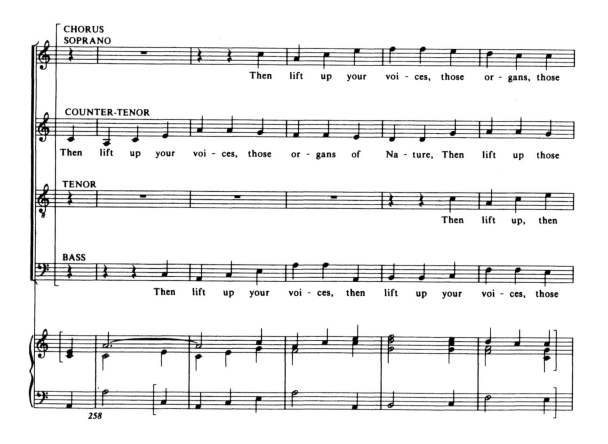

CHORUS
SOPRANO

Then lift up your voi - ces, those or - gans, those

COUNTER-TENOR

Then lift up your voi - ces, those or - gans of Na - ture, Then lift up those

TENOR

Then lift up, then

BASS

Then lift up your voi - ces, then lift up your voi - ces, those

258

charms to the trou - bled, those charms to the trou - bled and am - - o - rous crea - ture.

charms to the trou - bled, those charms to the trou - bled and am - - o - rous crea - ture.

charms to the_ trou - bled, those charms to the trou - bled and am - - o - rous crea - ture.

charms to the trou - - - - - - - - bled and am - - o - rous crea - ture.

275

281

TENOR SOLO

Beau - ty, thou scene of love, And_ Vir - tue, thou in - no - cent fire,

285

Made by the Pow-ers a-bove To__ tem-per the heat of de-sire,

291

-sire, Mu-sic, that Fan-cy em-ploys In rap-tures of in-no-cent

297

flame, We of-fer with lute and with voice To Ce-ci-lia, Ce-ci-lia's bright Name.

303

310

TENOR SOLO

In a con-sort of voi-ces while in-stru-ments play, With mu-sic we ce-le-brate

this ho - ly— day: I - ô Ce - ci - lia, Ce - ci - - - - - -

342

SOPRANO

CHORUS

In a con-sort of voi - - - - -

COUNTER-TENOR

In a con-sort of voi - ces while

TENOR

- lia,_ Ce - ci - lia, Ce - ci - lia.

In a con-sort of

BASS

In a

348

354

360

Published by Novello Publishing Limited
Music setting by Stave Origination